THE THREE FACES OF POWER

Other books by Adolf A. Berle

The Modern Corporation and Private Property
(with Gardiner C. Means)

Liquid Claims and National Wealth
(with Victoria J. Pederson)

The Natural Selection of Political Forces

The 20th Century Capitalist Revolution

Tides of Crisis

Power Without Property: A New Development in
American Political Economy

Latin America: Diplomacy and Reality

The American Economic Republic

ADOLF A. BERLE

THE
THREE FACES
OF
POWER

Harcourt, Brace & World, Inc.
New York

First edition

Library of Congress Catalog Card Number: 68–12565

These essays were originally presented as the
Carpentier Lectures at Columbia University in March 1967.

FOREWORD

This is a report on a revolution. The unique fact is that the revolutionary committee is the Supreme Court of the United States.

The first of the three essays relates to the acquisition and exercise by the Supreme Court of senior legislative power in the United States, particularly in the field of education and local government.

The second relates to a like power claimed by the Court over economic organization—large corporations —under the federal antitrust and other laws.

The third essay suggests a possible method of extricating the Court, in some measure, from the position of danger as well as honor it has acquired.

Use of the word "revolution" implies no criticism of the Court.[1] I think it could not have acted otherwise than as it did. Far from arrogating to itself powers it did not have, the Court's latent constitutional powers granted it

1. Associate Justice Abe Fortas of the Supreme Court: "It is fascinating, although disconcerting to some, that the first and fundamental breakthrough in various categories of *revolutionary progress* has been made by the courts—and specifically the Supreme Court of the United States." (James Madison Lecture at the New York University Law School, March 29, 1967, reported on the editorial page of the *New York Law Journal*, Wednesday, April 5, 1967. (Italics added.)

by the Fourteenth Amendment were activated by the
pace of technical and social change. When this history is
written, it will probably be found that the Supreme
Court's action saved the country from a far more dangerous and disorderly change.

Yet the situation does impose on the federal government problems of power which must be solved if the
Supreme Court is not to endanger or lose its mandate
through tides of political action. Revolutionary progress
does fuse judicial and legislative power, and possibly a
degree of executive power as well. A common sequel is
liquidation of that power as increasing sectors of opposition or fear become active. In the case of the Supreme
Court, some are evident now. Thirty-four states by legislative act have called for a constitutional convention, the
motive being to end the power of the Supreme Court
used in *Baker* v. *Carr*[2] as well as the result of that case.
Since the Congress, required to call the constitutional
convention, will probably resist, a first-class constitutional crisis could easily ensue with the Supreme Court
as its focus.

No apology is needed, accordingly, for raising or dis-
cussing the problem. As noted in the text, this writer is
in accord with what the Court did. He would merely like
to ease the transition which must inevitably ensue.

2. *Baker* v. *Carr,* 369 US 186 (1962).

CONTENTS

ix

THE THREE FACES OF POWER

I

THE SUPREME COURT OF THE UNITED STATES AS SENIOR HOLDER OF LEGISLATIVE POWER

Introduction: The Laws of Power

The thesis can be briefly stated. Ultimate legislative power in the United States has come to rest in the Supreme Court of the United States. As will presently appear, this broad statement of an unrecognized fact is not made in opposition. Given the social and economic revolution of the United States, I do not see that the Supreme Court could well have avoided the legislative position in which it now finds itself; and I am in accord with the results it has achieved. But the situation does require additional development making it possible for ultimate development providing for two inevitable problems. One of these is an institutional base for the gathering of data on which the legislative decrees of the federal courts may be soundly based. The second is provision for dealing with the political problems inevitably resulting from the use of legislative power.

By way of background, we must consider the subject of power itself. Unhappily, there is no accepted theory of power, though the subject has been discussed at least since the days of Plato's *Republic*. At present we are in about the situation of Adam Smith when, after general observation of the world, he outlined the theory of political economy embodied in *The Wealth of Nations*. After considerable study of the subject, I state as my own premise the apparent existence of five laws of power. In the case of the Supreme Court only the fifth is really involved, though the other four are necessary for background.

They are:

1. Power will invariably enter and organize any situation threatening chaos or disorder.

2. Power is always personal, coming to rest in a man or men.

3. Power is invariably supported by, and usually invested in, institutions, organizing its exercise and its application.

4. The institutions for the exercise and application of power are invariably based upon a philosophy or idea system.

5. The institutions of power and the power holders and the idea structure invariably are confronted by a field of responsibility, be it acknowledged and recognized or unrecognized and inchoate.

This field includes everyone conscious of being affected directly or indirectly by the consequences of the decisions or failure of decision of the power holders. The process of exercising (or failure to exercise) power sets up recognized or unrecognized dialogue between the power holders and the field of responsibility or segments of it.

Power obviously is not limited to emperors, presidents, Supreme Court justices, or heads of congressional committees. It is found in heads of corporations, heads of universities, deans of law schools, teachers in classrooms, heads of families. Observation will, I think, verify in fact that the five laws above stated apply in any of these situations, great or small. Clearly, the greater the situation, the greater the development of institutions, the idea systems on which they rest, the field of responsibility, and the resulting dialogue with it. Endeavor is here made to consider the present position of the Supreme Court of the United States in the light of these results.

Article I of the Constitution provides that

All legislative Powers herein granted shall be vested in a Congress of the United States, which shall consist of a Senate and House of Representatives.

Article III, Section 2, provides that

The judicial Power shall extend to all Cases, in Law and Equity, arising under this Constitution, the Laws of the United States, and Treaties made, or which shall be made, under their Authority.

Prima facie, this is no grant of legislative power to the Supreme Court. The Constitutional Convention accepted the doctrine of "separation of powers," the theory being that only by separating the legislative, the judicial, and the executive powers could a country preserve "a government of laws and not of men."

Thereafter, at the close of the Civil War, the Fourteenth Amendment was adopted, providing among other things that

No State shall make or enforce any law which shall abridge the privileges or immunities of citizens of the United States; nor shall any State deprive any person of life, liberty, or property, without due process of law; *nor deny to any person within its jurisdiction the equal protection of the laws.* [Italics added.]

At the time of adoption, protection of life, liberty, and property bulked very large in general thinking. "Equal protection of the laws" was a quite separate subject, potentially of far larger import, and took off from a desire that no institution like slavery should be permitted.[1]

The ensuing century saw a revolution in national habits, institutions, and social standards whose proportion we have yet to apprehend. Included in it was transition from an agricultural to an industrial society; the concentration of industry, transport and, to some extent, finance in the hands of a few hundred corporations; the concomitant concentration of power over wages, conditions of labor, and in large measure access to employment, in the hands of powerful labor unions. Following the catastrophe of 1933, the federal government assumed responsibility for the economic condition of the country

1. *Vide* Samuel Eliot Morison, *Oxford History of the American People,* New York, Oxford University Press, 1965, pp. 771–772. "The Supreme Court in 1873 declined to intervene between the state of Louisiana and the New Orleans butchers, who alleged that state regulations were confiscatory. The Court explained that Amendment XIV had been adopted to protect the freed slaves, not to make the federal judiciary 'a perpetual censor upon all legislation of the state . . . with authority to nullify such as it did not approve.' But this was before the judges began reading Herbert Spencer."

Dear Alumnus:

For those of you who were unable
to attend Professor Berle's
Carpentier Lectures, and for those
of you who were there and wish to
have them in published form, this
book is sent to you.

With it, go our best wishes and
continued appreciation for your
loyalty and support.

William C. Warren

and presently codified that responsibility in the Employment Act of 1946. Since this act is less well known than
it should be, I quote the key provision:

The Congress declares that it is the continuing policy and
responsibility of the Federal Government to use all practicable
means consistent with its needs and obligations and other essential considerations of national policy, with the assistance
and cooperation of industry, agriculture, labor, and State and
local governments, to coordinate and utilize all its plans, functions, and resources for the purpose of creating and maintain-
ing, in a manner calculated to foster and promote free competitive enterprise and the general welfare, conditions under
which there will be afforded useful employment opportunities,
including self-employment, for those able, willing, and seeking
to work, and to promote maximum employment, production,
and purchasing power. [15 USCA §1021]

Heightened responsibility and ensuing state and federal
action brought a vast body of state and federal legislation
into existence.

Thereafter (it is not wholly, but chiefly, a development since the close of World War II), the social-eco-
nomic operations of this complex organism we call the
United States made enormous progress.[2] The average of

2. See J. W. Kendricks, *The United States National Bureau of Eco-
nomics Review,* Princeton, Princeton University Press, New Jersey,
1961.
There is no single statement of the extent of technical change—
probably to make one would require an encyclopedia. An illuminating
essay is found in *The Changing American Economy,* edited by John
R. Coleman, New York, 1966, "Automation in Perspective," by
Lloyd Ulman, pp. 182–197. More technical—and of one extreme development—is the number of *Scientific American* for September
1966 devoted to computers and their use; among other things, tech-
nology, organization, and education. Anyone older than forty-five

personally received income moved from $1,491 per capita
in 1950 to an estimated $2,900 in 1967.[3] The country
learned that education was an essential part of this process. Recent studies summarized in *Sources of Economic
Growth* (Committee for Economic Development, 1962)
indicate that between 20% and 25% of the increase in
Gross National Product—and, of course, in personally received income—could be ascribed to expenditure for education. Presently a heightened social conscience led to
the current campaign to eliminate poverty—a campaign
which obviously will not abate though methods of attack
may change.[4] Attempt to give more or less equal access to
the benefits of medical knowledge and medical care is the
precise object of the recent statute providing for medical
aid.[5]

Other extensions of government responsibility are ap-
pearing over the horizon. The proposition that every
American family is unconditionally entitled to an income
of subsistence level has already been substantially supported. The immediate proposal—a "negative income
tax," supplying that income—may not be the solution

---

needs only look at the world around him—and remember his school
days.

3. *U.S. Book of Facts,* p. 334.

4. Surprisingly, the war on poverty is supported not only from the
side of the "poor," but also by the great corporations. The *Wall Street
Journal* of April 19, 1967 (p. 1) chronicles the appearance of executives of the following corporations in support of the "war on
poverty": General Electric, Hotel Company of America, Radio Corporation of America, U.S. Industries, Inc., Xerox Corporation, In-
ternational Business Machines Corporation, Montgomery Ward & Co.,
and a number of others.

5. "Medicare," Public Law 89–97, The Social Security Amendments
of 1965 (USCA Title 42).

eventually adopted,[6] but something like it has already appeared as the relief operations in the states slowly move away from the field of charity toward the field of economic right.

Let us revert to the Fourteenth Amendment. The field of the laws whose "equal protection" must not be denied to "any person" within the jurisdiction of "any State" has been vastly increased since—and is still being increased. At some point, the question was bound to arise, "What is 'equal protection' under the new conditions and concepts?"—as, of course, it had arisen under the more limited conceptions and provisions of laws existing at the time of its adoption.

When it did arise, the revolution began.

The first stage was square determination that the "equal protection of the laws" clause did not merely inhibit action by the states, it also required them to *create* a situation giving "equal protection." State "inaction" (as Justice Arthur Goldberg later observed) within the meaning of the Fourteenth Amendment was itself responsible state action. If a system existed which did not provide equal protection, then primarily the state or, if not the state, some other authority was obligated to create it.

The second stage of the revolution came when, faced with state "inaction," the federal courts assumed the task

6. It is by no means beyond possibility that in a couple of decades conception of "equal protection of the laws" may require enactment of a guaranteed income to everyone at some level. Presumably by that time everyone not enjoying an income will have some right to relief, or perhaps will be on a Social Security allowance. Might not the Supreme Court rule, first, that government (presumably federal) had already entered the field of guaranteeing most individuals against destitution and, second, therefore rule that failure to provide such protection for all denied equal protection?

of filling the vacuum, remedying the failure. In plain English, this meant undertaking by decree to enact the rules which state legislation has failed to provide. This second phase was the really revolutionary development—and, incidentally, set up the Supreme Court as a revolutionary committee.

As noted earlier, this statement is not made in criticism. I do not see that the Supreme Court could have done otherwise. By assuming the function, it is clear to me, the Court safeguarded the United States from an otherwise chaotic and dangerous situation which might have led to catastrophe.

1. Education

Historically, the moment was reached when the Supreme Court was presented with the case of *Brown* v. *Board of Education of Topeka*.[7] Chief Justice Earl Warren and a majority of the Court then decided that segregation of white from Negro children in state-maintained public schools denied Negroes "equal protection of the laws." At this point, predictably and I think unavoidably, the reserve legislative power of the Supreme Court became overt. The Supreme Court's lawmaking power in constitutional fields was implicit since adoption of the Fourteenth Amendment. Unquestionably it had been exercised before 1954. Legal historians may be left to discuss its slow emergence into general consciousness. Po-

7. *Brown* v. *Board of Education of Topeka*, 347 US 483 (1954).

litically, it can hardly be doubted that the *Brown* case pushed judicial legislation into public awareness. The school segregation cases brought the subject over the crest of the hill and there it certainly remains.

In my view, no other result was possible. The Constitution contemplated a court chiefly occupied with the specific solution of cases and controversies. In constitutional matters, its original and primary power was to say "No"—that is, to strike down statutes and administrative or judicial actions violating the Bill of Rights amendments or taken outside the power granted to legislatures or executive officials, or trespassing on the division of powers between the federal and state governments. Seven of the ten Bill of Rights amendments are cast in the negative: "The Congress shall make no law respecting establishment of religion"; "The right of the people to keep and bear arms shall not be infringed," and so forth. In most of these cases, "nay" saying is very nearly sufficient. Capacity to strike down the offending rule or action covers most cases. Positive requirements were set up chiefly in respect of procedure: "The accused shall enjoy the right to a speedy and public trial"; "The right of trial by jury shall be preserved," and the like. These relate specifically to judicial procedure, clearly under the control of the courts.

But consider the Fourteenth Amendment: "No State shall . . . deny to any person within its jurisdiction the equal protection of the laws." The double negative effects a highly positive command. "Equal protection of the laws" often cannot be created by the mere strike-down of an offending provision. An implacable dialectic emerges.

Here is a scheme of laws. The Court must decide whether
it denies equal protection. Power to say "No" in some
situations inevitably implies power to say "Yes" in others.
Joined to the conceded equity power giving the Court
capacity to decree a remedy, a question comes up in each
case. Unless prepared to draw a decree itself, the Court
may, and in practice must, remand the case to the lower
court with instructions to draw a decree creating a situation in which the aggrieved party will have equal protection. A mere negative decree is likely to create a frag-
ment of unfilled chaos. If the federal courts do not prescribe positive action, the Court's decision is likely to be
brutum fulmen.

The narrow issue before the Supreme Court in *Brown*
v. *Topeka* (the school segregation cases) was whether it
or the lower federal courts should undertake to remedy
the wrongs complained of by decree. Any such decree
would be legislative in character, with sweeping results.
The Court might have evaded in some fashion both decision and decree-making, as Justice Felix Frankfurter on
various occasions urged that it do.[8] His forecast of the
thickets and difficulties into which the Court would be
plunged was unquestionably accurate. Nevertheless, I
think he was wrong. To have abstained from dealing with
the issues presented would have produced a chaotic rather
than an orderly revolution. Especially in race discrimination cases, abstention would have thrown the issue straight
to the streets in a number of localities—and only an

8. First, in *Railroad Commission* v. *Pullman Company,* 312 US 496
(1941). For the history of abstention, see *Harvard Law Review,*
Vol. 80, No. 3 (Jan. 1967, pp. 604 ff.).

omniscient deity can tell what then would have happened. When Chief Justice Warren grasped the nettle in *Brown* v. *Topeka* and thereafter, he was entitled, not to a call for his impeachment, as some extremists have done, but to the public thanks of the United States. The Chief Justice was revolutionary. But he was right.

Latent in his decision was whether the Fourteenth Amendment set up an *affirmative* requirement to provide "equal protection" and, if so, whether its mandate required action by the Supreme Court. Impliedly, at least, the Court determined the former—the Fourteenth Amendment required the states to set up an "equal protection" system, and that requirement could be enforced by the courts. The Court did not explicitly so decide, until the problem was forthrightly dealt with in *Bell* v. *Maryland*.[9] In *Bell*, Justice Goldberg (joined by Chief Justice Warren) quoted correspondence of Justice Joseph P. Bradley, who had decided the civil-rights cases in 1876, as saying:

denying [equal protection] includes inaction as well as action, and denying the equal protection of the laws includes the omission to protect, as well as the omission to pass laws for protection,

and Justice Goldberg added:

These views are fully consonant with this Court's recognition that state conduct which might be described as "inaction" can nevertheless constitute responsible "state action" within the meaning of the Fourteenth Amendment.

9. *Bell* v. *Maryland,* 378 US 226, 309–310 (1964).

It is difficult to believe that the Chief Justice in *Brown* v. *Topeka* did not recognize the course of probability. The Supreme Court, under the Fourteenth Amendment, would be called on not only to strike down discriminatory laws, but also to *create* nondiscriminatory conditions— and that involved the probability of judicial legislation on an extremely wide front.

Probably no one was more aware of the implications than was Chief Justice Warren himself. The Court unanimously determined several propositions: first, that

where the State has undertaken to provide [public education], it is a right which must be made available to all on equal terms;[10]

second, that, in the light of modern knowledge, segregation had a tendency to retard the educational and mental development of Negro children and deprive them of some of the benefits they would receive in a rationally integrated school system,[11] and, third, that the doctrine of "separate but equal facilities" had no place in public education, because it deprived Negro children of "equal protection of the laws." [12]

The Chief Justice at least impliedly accepted the fact

10. *Brown* v. *Topeka,* at p. 493.

11. Note ought to be made of a point involved in the Supreme Court ruling. Clearly, Negro children are entitled to education equal to that provided for whites. Whether a "racially" integrated school system necessarily affords that is matter of educational judgment. Quite possibly a generation hence educators may consider that children up to, say, the age of ten receive better education if in a group of children wholly familiar to them than in a group with mixed or diverse backgrounds and habits. A point of educational dogma was accepted by the Court; behavioral science may later shift the conclusion.

12. *Brown* v. *Topeka,* at p. 494.

that the Court's ruling was legislative in character. Because of the wide applicability of this decision, and because of the great variety of local conditions, framing the orders presented problems of considerable complexity.[13] The Court therefore restored the case to the docket for argument on the formulation of decrees—and directed that the Attorney General of the United States and the attorneys general of those states requiring or permitting segregation be invited to appear as *amici curiae*. In other words, the Court determined the principles of the legislation, and called a hearing to determine its exact terms. Mere injunction prohibiting race segregation without more would have accomplished nothing.

2.   The Legislative Power Widens

Though the school segregation cases were and perhaps still are the most spectacular exercise of legislative power, they are only one sector of a great and growing number of such cases. Description of all of them would require a volume; a few illustrations will suggest part of their scope.

The Tennessee Legislature in 1901 provided that the General Assembly should be composed of thirty-three senators and ninety-nine representatives, to be apportioned among the various counties. Some of these elected one representative, others elected two, three, six, or eight representatives. The least populous counties were grouped into blocs, and two, three, and four counties jointly

13. *Ibid.*, at p. 495.

elected one representative. A somewhat similar scheme
determined election of senators.

No change in apportionment was made between 1901
and 1960, by which time the population of Tennessee
had increased from 2 million to 3½ million, and the
population eligible to vote from 487,000 to 2,100,000.
As might be expected, the county growth was not uniform, so that

37% of the voters of Tennessee elect 20 of the 33 Senators
while 40% of the voters elect 63 of the 99 members of the
House.[14]

Justice Tom Clark later observed that

the apportionment picture in Tennessee is a topsy-turvical of
gigantic proportions. . . . Tennessee's apportionment is a
crazy quilt without rational basis.[15]

In *Baker* v. *Carr,* a group of voters brought action in
the federal court asking relief from denial of "equal protection of the laws" because they were virtually deprived
of opportunity to cast a meaningful vote. The lower
court dismissed the complaint, and appeal was taken.
The plaintiffs not only asked that the Tennessee apportionment be ruled unconstitutional; they also asked
an injunction preventing further elections from being
held under it and

unless and until the General Assembly enacts a valid reapportionment, the District Court should either decree a reapportionment by mathematical application of the Tennessee

14. *Baker* v. *Carr,* at p. 707.
15. *Ibid.*

constitutional formulae to the most recent Federal Census figures, or direct the appellees to conduct legislative elections, primary and general, at large.[16]

The Court decided that disparity of representation was indeed a denial of "equal protection of the laws," and that decision of the cause ought not to be avoided by describing it as a "political question" to be left to some other branch of government. Graceful bow was made to the doctrine of "separation of powers," but the Court found no difficulty in crossing that Rubicon. A state exercising power wholly within the domain of state interest is insulated from federal judiciary review. But where state power is an instrument for circumventing a federally protected right, the federal courts may move in (*Gomillion* v. *Lightfoot*, 364 US 339).

So the Supreme Court, against the warning of Justice Frankfurter,[17] moved in. It declared the principle of "one man–one vote," deciding that irrational and discriminatory apportionment of voting power denied "equal protection of the laws"—and that the Tennessee Legislature was badly elected.

But then what? The majority of the Court merely re-

16. *Ibid.,* p. 673.

17. "A hypothetical claim resting on abstract assumptions is now for the first time made the basis for affording illusory relief for a particular evil even though it foreshadows deeper and more pervasive difficulties in consequence. The claim is hypothetical and the assumptions are abstract because the Court does not vouchsafe the lower courts—state and federal—guidelines for formulating specific, definite, wholly unprecedented remedies for the inevitable litigations that today's umbrageous disposition is bound to stimulate in connection with politically motivated reapportionments in so many States" (*Ibid.,* at p. 715).

manded the cause to the lower, three-judge, court for
appropriate action without attempting to formulate remedy. Justice Clark disliked this, believing that appropriate
remedy should be formulated by the Supreme Court itself. In a concurring opinion, he suggested a formula.
Justice John Marshall Harlan did likewise, though his
formula was different. Justice Frankfurter prophesied
doom and gloom, partly because he thought the Supreme
Court had no business in this area, and partly because it
gave no guidance to the lower court on how to enforce
the new requirement. He considered that the lower courts
of the country had been catapulted into a "mathematical
quagmire . . . without so much as adumbrating the
basis for a legal calculus as a means of extrication." [18]

In effect [continued Justice Frankfurter], today's decision em-
powers the courts of the country to devise what should constitute the proper composition of the legislatures of the fifty
States. If state courts should for one reason or another find
themselves unable to discharge this task, the duty of doing so
is put on the federal courts or on this Court, if State views do
not satisfy this Court's notion of what is proper districting.[19]

Frankfurter wanted to abstain from the whole affair,
acknowledging that

there is not under our Constitution a judicial remedy for every
political mischief, for every undesirable exercise of legislative
power.[20]

18. *Ibid.*
19. *Ibid.,* at p. 716.
20. *Ibid.*

The Court's judgment in remanding the cause to the district court for "further proceedings consistent with this opinion" meant, in practice, either persuading the state legislature to reapportion or decreeing reapportionment itself.

Justice Frankfurter's premonitions were not wholly unjustified, though the problems he foresaw have not yet proved insoluble. A string of cases demanding reapportionment was immediately brought, and all manner of problems were raised thereby.[21] Surprisingly, solutions

21. In *Reynolds* v. *Sims,* 377 US 533 (1964), the apportionment of legislators in Alabama was challenged on the ground that the urban counties were unrepresented. A three-judge federal court (United States District Court for the Middle District of Alabama) ordered a temporary reapportionment. On direct appeal, the Supreme Court of the United States affirmed; Clark concurring. Justice Potter Stewart supported his concurrence because the three-judge decree afforded "the State of Alabama full opportunity, consistent with the requirements of the Federal Constitution, to devise its own system of legislative apportionment" (at p. 543). Justice Harlan, dissenting, said— accurately as it proved: "The consequence of today's decision is that in all but the handful of States which may already satisfy the new requirements the local District Court or, it may be, the state courts, are given blanket authority and the constitutional duty to supervise apportionment of the State Legislatures. It is difficult to imagine a more intolerable and inappropriate interference by the judiciary with the independent legislatures of the States" (at p. 558).

Since the Supreme Court decision in *Reynolds* v. *Sims* requiring that elections to state legislatures assure the rights of all citizens "to cast an effective and adequately weighted vote" (at p. 581), the principle has been carried into county government. There are presently pending in *the courts of New York alone,* cases affecting the following counties: Albany, Broome, Chemung, Clinton, Dutchess, Erie, Genesee, Herkimer, Monroe, Oneida, Onondaga, Rockland (in the federal as well as the New York Supreme Court), St. Lawrence, Saratoga, Schenectady, Seneca, Steuben, Suffolk (before a federal court), Sullivan, Ulster, Washington, Westchester (litigation in the federal as well as in the state courts).

have generally been reached. The legislative decrees of
the federal courts in general have worked out, though at
times the results have been surprising.

One example was the situation in New York.

A group of citizens residing in the most populous
counties of New York brought suit challenging the apportionment for electing state assemblymen and state
senators. A three-judge federal district court dismissed
the case on the ground that the apportionment did not
violate the United States Constitution. The Supreme
Court of the United States, by six to three, reversed this
decision; it said that the "equal protection" clause requires
both houses of the state legislature to be apportioned
substantially on a population base—as they were not in
New York. Again the case was remanded to the court
below for further proceedings, though the dissenters in
the Court thought the majority wrong and suggested
alternative affirmative plans.

The New York Legislature thereupon adopted four
alternative plans and submitted them to the federal district court for approval. Three were thrown out at once;
the district court thought that the fourth satisfied constitutional requirements. Meanwhile, in simultaneous litigation in the New York state courts, the New York Court
of Appeals, applying the state constitution, considered
the plans proposed by the state legislature and held all
four of them bad.[22] The fourth—the plan approved by

22. See *WMCA* v. *Lomenzo, Secretary of State of the State of New
York,* 377 US 633 (1964). Five of New York's most populous counties challenged the apportionment of the legislature in New York. A
three-judge court dismissed the complaint (208 F. Supp. 368). On
appeal, the Supreme Court of the United States reversed. During the

the federal district court—required election of more state assemblymen than the constitution of the State of New York allowed. Appeal was taken from the district court decision, but, in *Travia* v. *Lomenzo*,[23] the Supreme Court by memorandum dismissed the appeal. Justice Harlan, dissenting, plaintively observed that the Supreme Court ignored the fact that the New York Court of Appeals held that *Plan A* (the plan approved by the federal district court) violated the state constitution—as it plainly did— but he got nowhere. So *Plan A* became effective in the State of New York, and a legislature of the State of New York was elected under an apportionment scheme decreed by the federal court with an assembly containing more members than the state constitution allowed.[24] For

litigation, a similar challenge was made in the New York courts. The Supreme Court of the United States reversed the district court and recommended further proceedings consistent with the Court's view expressed in *Reynolds* v. *Sims* and in its opinion in this case.

This time Justices Stewart and Clark joined with Harlan in dissenting—they had concurred in the earlier cases, though for other reasons. Justice Stewart said: "I am convinced these decisions mark a long step backward into that unhappy era when a majority of the members of this Court were thought by many to have convinced themselves and each other that the demands of the Constitution were to be measured not by what it says, but by their own notions of wise political theory" (p. 584), and denied states the right of experimentation.

23. *Travia* v. *Lomenzo,* 381 US 431 (1965).

24. *Travia* v. *Lomenzo.* In *Scott* v. *Germano,* 381 US 407 (1965), the United States District Court for the Northern District of Illinois declared the Illinois Senate invalidly apportioned and directed that if a valid plan were not submitted, the Court would require all parties to show cause why the next Illinois Legislature should not be elected at large. On appeal, the Court vacated the district court's order because the Supreme Court of Illinois had also held the apportionment invalid. The Supreme Court said that the United States District Court should

practical purposes, the federal district court supervised by
the Supreme Court of the United States briefly became the
legislative, perhaps even constitution-making, authority
of New York. Other similar cases have been in litigation
elsewhere in the United States.

The impact and the political importance of the holding
in *Baker* v. *Carr* and subsequent cases are very nearly
unlimited. Effectively, it calls for transfer of control of
legislatures in many states from the sparsely inhabited,
overrepresented agricultural counties to the previously
underrepresented large cities and urban regions. There-
tofore relatively small numbers of farmers and voters in
small towns were final arbiters of legislation. Hereafter,
the elected representatives of the urbanized masses will
become the arbiters instead. Change in point of view as
well as in economic interest must inevitably take place—
indeed, has done so already.

Revolutions have been fought for less fundamental
changes in power structure.

3.   Other Fields of Revolution

The two illustrations given in some detail are merely the
more dramatic of a series of lesser changes stemming
from the same root. They are here mentioned rather than
described.

---

have "stayed its hand," and directed the district court to fix "a reasonable time within which the appropriate agencies of the State of
Illinois, including its Supreme Court, may validly redistrict the Illinois State Senate" in time for the elections of 1966 (p. 409).

ened by 3%; therefore a merger could be prohibited. Looking into the subject further, the growth of a number of companion ideas can be discovered. Mere size may in itself constitute a limitation of competition. So perhaps may expansion of a corporation into a number of unrelated fields. There is under consideration in the Department of Justice an attack on a corporation on the ground that the massiveness of its advertising, in and of itself, may diminish or preclude effective competition— as indeed it may.

It has long been established by law that when a corporation is found to have violated the Sherman Antitrust Act or the Clayton Act, the federal courts may prescribe a remedy—prohibiting practice, ordering divestiture of properties, or dissolving the defendant corporation. In practice, the Court then prescribes the extent and outline of the company's organization. If, through the gate of determining what is "competition," the Court undertakes to determine the limits of size, of ownership of diverse operations, of advertising, it will move yet more deeply into regulation of the organization and conduct of American business. The blanket of "interstate commerce" now covers most of that field. The mental constructs of the Supreme Court—its conception of "competition," of advertising, of the dangers of size, of the dangers of lessening competition where size is not the major consideration —of necessity could become the senior controls over American business.

In another field, the First Amendment to the Constitution, prohibiting Congress from making any law "abridging the freedom of speech, or of the press," taken together with the Fourteenth Amendment, has already led

In the field of industrial organization, court-made r
lution is becoming as evident as in the fields of educat.
and state government. Long ago, the Sherman Antitru
Act was given quasi-constitutional standing by the Supreme Court of the United States.[25] In due time, it was
implemented by the Clayton Act,[26] which in turn was
amended to permit governmental intervention preventing
mergers whose effect was to "substantially lessen competition." [27] But any contract by which supplies are bought or
sold from or to a particular party over a period of time
lessens competition. Whether the lessening is "substantial"
is a matter of opinion.[28] In due time, the Supreme Court
moved into the picture and asserted its opinion by deciding *Brown Shoe Company* v. *United States.*[29] It there held
that in certain "relevant markets" competition was less-

25. *Appalachian Coals Company* v. *United States,* 288 US 344 (1932),
at pp. 359–360. "As a charter of freedom, the Act has a generality and
adaptability comparable to that found to be desirable in constitutional
provisions," wrote Chief Justice Charles Evans Hughes. The statement has often been repeated; see *U.S.* v. *E. I. Dupont de Nemours
& Company,* 361 US 381 (1956) at p. 386. Whether Chief Justice
Hughes intended to go as far as his successors may be questioned—
but there is no doubt of the result.

26. Act of October 15, 1914. Chap. 323, 15 USCA §§12, 13, 14–21,
22–27.

27. 15 USCA §18 as amended by Act of December 29, 1950, to prohibit the acquisition of the whole or any part of the assets of another
corporation, when the effect of the acquisition may substantially
lessen competition or tend to create a monopoly.

28. Later, in *Federal Trade Commission* v. *Procter & Gamble Company,* the Supreme Court was to rule that the merger of the two non-
competitive companies, creating large market power, might substantially limit competition if the merged companies decided to compete
in other fields, and insisted that prediction rather than proof must
necessarily enter into the decision. This goes pretty far.

29. *Brown Shoe Company* v. *United States,* 370 US 294 (1962).

to a rewriting of much of the law of libel and slander. Justice William O. Douglas maintains, and the Supreme Court has held, that an individual in public life, and particularly an officeholder, is entitled to no protection whatever. If one's life lies in the public domain, he argues, comment or characterization of it must be free. In result, however malicious, mendacious, or outrageous a slander may be, a person in public life has no redress at law. A widely advertised play, *MacBird,* may be cited as illustration. Regrettably, other redress, such as access to mass or other media assuring scope of answer equal to the scope of attack, has not yet been worked out—though it is not difficult to imagine that just such countervailing right might be developed in future judicial decisions.

Two years ago, in *Schneider* v. *Rusk,*[30] the Court had before it a federal statute providing that a naturalized citizen lost nationality if he resided continuously for three years in the foreign state of which he was formerly a national. A majority of the Court held the statute bad as a discrimination against naturalized citizens under the Fifth Amendment—although similar clauses and naturalization treaties had contained similar provisions for nearly a century.

4. The Essential Problem

My concern is not with the merits of the decisions reached by the courts, though in general I agree with them. My concern lies elsewhere.

30. *Schneider* v. *Rusk,* 377 US 163 (1965).

This revolution, like others, has had as its first effect a tremendous concentration of power—in this case, in the hands of the Supreme Court of the United States. That was the result of erecting the Fourteenth Amendment into a command that states shall create conditions satisfying the requirements of "equal protection." Standards of "equal protection" change with time and conditions, as Chief Justice John Marshall long ago foresaw they would.[31] In the past half-century, conditions and concepts have changed, perhaps more rapidly than in any similar period in recorded history. The Supreme Court considers—and the American public accepts its view—that it has the power and the duty to determine when these changes impose new or different obligations on the states. If a case is brought before it, the new conditions can be assessed, new obligations imposed by judicial command, and new implementation required by the federal courts—unless state action makes this unnecessary. The discussions of the Court in *Bell* v. *Maryland* were essentially debates in a revolutionary assembly. The only odd circumstance is to find them taking place in a court.

The dialectic imposed by the present interpretation of the Fourteenth Amendment inexorably pushes the Court into the causative and essentially legislative position it now holds. Given the degree of change, the manner and method of this judicial revolution were perhaps the least costly and most effective possible under the circumstances. Revolutions have been going forward all over the world, many of them at the cost of endless bloodshed,

31. *McCulloch* v. *Maryland,* 4 Wheaton 316, 407 (1819).

disorder, and human misery. Without its judicial revolution, the United States might have encountered like periods of chaos.

Yet every revolution is eventually faced with the problem of relocating power and providing it with sustaining institutions. That has been true at least since the days of Oliver Cromwell. This problem, it seems to me, the Supreme Court and the federal political and legal systems must presently solve. Thinking along that line had best be done before the problem becomes acute, and no apology is needed for raising the question now.

Specifically, an institutional solution must be devised which will, first, indicate the areas in which the system of laws prevailing has failed to give "equal protection"; and where action is needed. Second, orderly mechanism must be provided for having the problems thus developed placed before the appropriate political bodies for action. Third, the Supreme Court itself should be persuaded to require that political action through the Congress and the legislatures should be sought before the Court's decree-making and judicial legislative power be invoked. Judicial legislation should be availed of as an ultimate and emergency power rather than as standard operating procedure. In the third essay we shall explore possibilities of doing this, in the hope that, after the Court quite justifiably assumed the powers of a revolutionary committee, these powers may be redevolved in orderly fashion on the institutions devised to deal with them.

Reverting to our five original laws of power, it appears that the Supreme Court asserted its power to prevent a potentially chaotic situation; that it found a fairly well-

defined idea system or philosophy embodied in the Constitution and the history of American democracy; and that
it utilized the system of federal courts as an institutional
framework giving effect to its decrees. So far, so good.

II

REVOLUTION IN ECONOMIC ORGANIZATION

Revolution, as we have seen, is already well under way in the fields of education and local government. Less evidently but no less surely it is taking place in the field of economic organization, now intensified by mechanics and cybernetics. Here the process has been slower and less obvious, but that is because our chief means of economic organization—the corporation—for some decades has already been a revolutionary instrument of the first order. That its development should force change in power relationships as well as legal concepts is hardly remarkable.

1.   The Background

Agriculture aside, most of the business of the United States, where it is not carried on by the government, is carried on by corporations—to be specific, about

1,200,000 of them, big and small. But four-fifths or more
of the total activity is carried on by about 3,500 corporations in all, whose stock is listed respectively on the New
York Stock Exchange, the American Stock Exchange, or
the over-the-counter markets. Even this is not a fair index.
Eight hundred corporations probably account for between
70% and 75% of all American business activity; 250
corporations account for perhaps two-thirds of it. These
figures do not take into account the fact that great numbers of smaller concerns are in effect, though not tech-
nically, controlled by their large associates. Thousands
of gasoline stations and automobile dealers in the United
States are nominally independent; practically, most of
their decisions are predetermined by supply arrangements, franchise contracts, or agency agreements with
the large corporations whose oil or cars or gadgets they
sell. Far and away the major part of the American supply-
and-exchange system is constituted of a few hundred (at
most) clusters of corporate enterprises, each of whose
major decisions are determined by a central giant.

Simultaneously—and, oddly enough, exactly contrary
to a famous prediction by Karl Marx—these aggregations
have not proved machines for accumulating personal
wealth. They have, it is true, accumulated productive
assets, tangible and intangible, to a degree staggering
imagination.[1] But they split the personal-wealth factor

1. American Telephone & Telegraph Company is currently estimated
to have approximately $30 billion of liquid and tangible assets. Gen-
eral Motors' assets are said to be in the vicinity of $20 billion; Stand-
ard Oil of New Jersey, about $11½ billion—to name only a few.
And 1,119 companies had total assets of $269.4 billion (*News Front,*
August, 1966, p. 49).

from the productive factor. (That is the real rationale of corporate stock.) But corporate stock has been increasingly distributed rather than accumulated. Directly, there may be 23 million owners of stock in the United States. Indirectly, through pension and similar funds, some 30 or 40 million more Americans have a beneficial interest in the market value assigned by share quotations to the accumulated corporate assets—and a still more direct interest in the income generated and partly distributed by them. At least one-third of personally owned wealth in the United States is now held in the form of stock. The erstwhile village blacksmith would today be an employee in, say, Cyclops Steel, and would own a few shares of stock in the concern or have an interest in its pension fund.

Meantime, the United States has come to rely on the corporate organization for supply of most of its goods and a substantial part of its services, including the most essential of both—to say nothing of the fact that a substantial amount of employment is expected to be maintained by this system.[2]

The result—this one without intervention of the courts —was to bring about a minor revolution in itself. The

2. The effect of corporate policies on employment goes far beyond direct employment in plants or offices. The recession of 1956 was in part due to the fact that the three principal automobile manufacturers, General Motors, Ford, and Chrysler, sold 8 million cars in the previous year. *The National City Bank Economic Review* estimated the "normal" market for cars at the time at 6 million. The following year the motorcar companies sold only 4 million cars, and, naturally, purchased far less from their suppliers of raw materials, glass, et cetera. The effect on employment was severe.

classic ownership relation between men and producing
assets has been dissolved. Instead, men hold jobs—protected by labor unions and the National Labor Relations Board; and they own, directly or indirectly, pieces
of paper carrying expectation of dividends, with salability
provided by stock markets whose operations are federally
regulated under the Securities Act and a widening jurisdiction of the federal courts under Rule 10-b-5 of the
Securities and Exchange Commission. (That rule, it may
be noted, was made not by a legislature, but by an administrative commission, and it is more often cited than
the statute itself.)[3]

Because all this was happening—the statistics are staggering—none need be surprised that the underlying institution—the corporation—is at length coming in for
revolutionary judicial overhaul. Examination of this
movement is our present task. Perhaps we may also be
able to peer into the future.

2.   What Is a Corporation?

First among the problems raised is that of the real nature
of the corporation. What is a corporation, anyhow? I
do not wish to raise here the historic, hoary, and roman-
tic problem of the mystic corporate entity: though that
subject has intrigued authors for more than a century,

3. William L. Cary, *Politics and the Regulatory Agencies,* New York,
McGraw-Hill, 1965.

with roots going back to the days of *Sutton's Case*,[4] if
not before. Rather, I want to examine a more modern
question: Is a corporation a "person" within the purview
of the Fifth and Fourteenth Amendments? If not, what
are the consequences?

Until a few years ago, the question would have been
laughed at. In 1889, Justice Stephen J. Field, in *Minneapolis Railway Company* v. *Beckwith*,[5] formally held that

Corporations can invoke the benefits of provisions of the Constitution and laws which guarantee to persons the enjoyment
of property, or afford to them the means for its protection.

That was that for nearly three-fourths of a century.

Fifty years later, a routine case came along—*Connecticut General Life Insurance Company* v. *Johnson*.[6]
The State of California had undertaken to tax reinsurance
contracts, made in Connecticut, designed to indemnify
other insurance companies for losses on policies written
in California. This was attacked as being in violation of
the Fourteenth Amendment. Chief Justice Harlan Stone,
writing for the majority of the Court, held the California
tax bad under the Fourteenth Amendment. Dissenting,
Justice Hugo Black let drive at the basic doctrine. He
said the language and history of the amendment did "not
support the theory that it was passed for the benefit of
corporations," [7] and that the amendment applied only

4. *Sutton's Case*, 10 CO. 1 (1612). See, for one of many discussions
of it, 21 *Harvard Law Review*, p. 305 (1908).

5. *Minneapolis Railway Company* v. *Beckwith*, 129 US 26 (1889).

6. *Connecticut General Life Insurance Company* v. *Johnson*, 303 US
77 (1938).

7. *Ibid.*, pp. 86, 87.

to natural, not artificial, persons.[8] Glumly, he noted that
of the cases before the Supreme Court to which the Fourteenth Amendment was applied during the first fifty years
after its adoption, more than 50% asked that its benefits
be extended to corporations—and only one-half of 1%
invoked it in protection of the Negro race, for whose
protection this amendment was primarily designed.

Justice Black's was a single voice crying unnoticed
in the wilderness. A few years later, however, Justice
Douglas joined him (see *Wheeling Steel Company* v.
Glander),[9] and in 1964, in *Bell* v. *Maryland,* he returned
to the charge. There, the restaurant invoking police protection against Negro sit-ins was a corporation. The
Attorney General of Maryland, arguing in support of
their conviction, somewhat incautiously suggested that
the restaurant owner was a "person" having the right to
choose the parties with whom it would deal—a right
analogous to that of opening or closing the door of one's
home. This was Justice Douglas's opportunity, and he
drove at the whole conception of analogizing corporate
personality and individual personality. To his concurring
opinion he attached a series of appendices, four of which

8. See Clarence Cyril Walton and R. S. F. Eells, *The Business System,* New York, Macmillan, 1967, p. 1679, quoting from Woodrow
Wilson, "The Lawyer and the Community" (Report of the 33d Annual
Meeting of The American Bar Association, 1910, pp. 426–431). Wilson
said: "I regard the corporation as indispensable to modern business
enterprise. I am not jealous of its size or might, if you will but
abandon at the right points the fatuous, antiquated, and quite unnecessary fiction which treats it as a legal person; if you will but
cease to deal with it by means of your law as if it were a single individual not only, but also—what every child may perceive it is not—
a responsible individual."

9. *Wheeling Steel Company* v. *Glander,* 337 US 562 (1949).

were designed to show that most restaurants were oper-
ated by corporation chains, and that corporations were
not "individuals" either in fact or in law. Giving them
the status of individuals, guaranteeing them rights of
privacy in the use of their business property, would in
effect give them power through intracorporate regulation
to determine practices in race relations. Not only was
any property devoted to business not "private" in the
individual property sense, but also, if in corporate hands,
it was not "personal" property at all. He renewed his
head-on stricture of the ancient doctrine of *Minneapolis
Railway Company* v. *Beckwith* and powerfully reaffirmed
his position and Justice Black's that corporations were
not "persons" entitled to the protection of the Fourteenth
Amendment.

It so happens that as matter of history, of sociology,
and even of verbal interpretation, the Black-Douglas argument is unanswerable. The Fourteenth Amendment
was designed to protect natural persons; no other interpretation can be given the language. Sociologically, a
corporation, especially a large corporation, is anything
but a natural person. Legally, the fiction of its personality
has already been punctured. A corporation, for example,
does not have the privilege of self-incrimination guaranteed by the Fifth Amendment.[10] Attempt to give it the
quality of a natural person is patent nonsense.

Despite that, mere removal of the corporation from
Fourteenth Amendment protection does not answer all
the range of questions. The corporation may not be itself
a person. But it certainly is a composite of natural per-

10. *United States* v. *White*, 322 US 694, 698 (1944).

sons. These may be few—as in a close corporation—or
may run into millions—as in the case of the American
Telephone & Telegraph Company (actually 3,089,600,
according to its 1966 report). If we disregard the fictional
personality of a corporation and withdraw from it the
protections of the Fifth and Fourteenth Amendments, we
are still obliged to consider the individuals comprised in
the composite. They do have rights. It is scarcely arguable that by yielding part of their property to a corporation through the stockholding device, they have *pro tanto*
surrendered it out of all constitutional protection. Were
that to happen, some 22 million personal stockholders[11]
and 30 or 40 million holders of pension rights would
find themselves outside the constitutional system.

We have to look, therefore, beyond the immediate effect of the Black-Douglas doctrine—the more so because
I believe that doctrine will eventually prevail. Possibly
the corporation as a Fourteenth Amendment "person"
will vanish. But behind it will appear aggregates of natural persons, each one of whom does have a relationship
to the corporation, as employee, or as holder of a property interest in it. As to their interests, they are entitled
not to be deprived of "property" without due process of
law. They are even entitled not to be denied "equal protection of the laws" or the protections guaranteed by the
Bill of Rights.

11. Of the personally owned property held by citizens of the United
States, between one-fourth and one-third consists of corporation securities, chiefly stocks. The consensus of stockholders in 1965 showed
19,963,000 individual shareowners; the number has subsequently increased. See *New York Stock Exchange 1965 Consensus of Shareholders–Share Ownership U.S.A.*

"Personality" of the corporation was a fiction, and for Fourteenth Amendment purposes perhaps can be dispensed with. Yet the fact remains that a corporation is a composite of natural persons; these do have property interests entrusted by them to corporate managements. Justice Douglas was right in asserting that their individual "personality" did not carry over into the corporation. Ordinarily, the corporation could not set itself up as representing them in assertion of their individual or combined rights of privacy. On the other hand, a corporation, though not a "person" under the Fourteenth Amendment, not only can, but should and must, defend their combined property interests. Savings of individuals, directly represented by their stockholdings or indirectly represented through some $80 billion of pension trust funds held for their benefit, do mean a great deal to them, and are entitled to be represented and defended by the composite organism.

If the Black-Douglas doctrine prevails—as in logic it eventually should—I suggest that a rule suggests itself. The corporation would have standing to represent and defend the aggregate of individual rights held by or entrusted to the corporation. These ordinarily would be the property rights of shareholders; perhaps also the contract or other rights created through bargains reached collectively with employees; possibly even rights under agency and other arrangements reached in agreement with, let us say, salesmen and dealers.

The corporation, as such, would not be entitled to any of the constitutional rights that inhere in individual persons: the right to privacy or the like. Yet it would seem

that a corporation should be protected and should be
allowed to maintain (as corporations successfully have)
actions to defend such rights in representation of individuals within or as part of its operations.[12] For example,
a corporate newspaper or broadcasting company should
be protected as the defender of the right to freedom of
speech of the composite of its reporters and editorial
writers who had exercised that right through the corporate medium. An incorporated school or university
should have like right to defend the freedom of speech
of the composite of its faculty, students, and research
workers or any of them.

It is entirely arguable that while a corporation can
have no religion, if it is organized by men to carry forward religious purposes, their personal freedom of religion must be respected under the First Amendment
and may be protected through appropriate protection of
the corporation's activities. There seems no reason to
"abridge" freedom of speech because it is exercised
through the corporate form.

The problem in each case would be to determine
whether there is a personal right entitled to defense and,
second, whether the right can properly be defended or

12. In older conceptions, the corporation was considered a "trust" or
fiduciary for its shareholders. The conception is still valid. It would
seem that the corporation had not only the right, but also the duty
to defend the interests of the individuals for whose property it was
responsible—irrespective of whether it had "personality" or not. The
difficulty would lie in distinguishing between the interests of its shareholders and the interest of the corporation as a whole. Probably on
analysis it would appear that where the interest of the corporation
validly could be invaded or constricted through police power, regulation, and the like, the individuals as individuals would not be protected either.

asserted on behalf of the individuals by the composite we call a corporation.

So I do not see that the demise of the rule of *Minneapolis Railway Company* v. *Beckwith* and of the doctrine that corporations are "persons" within the meaning of the Bill of Rights would be any great disaster. Rather, it might clarify the situation.

3. Corporate Regulations as "Laws" under the Fourteenth Amendment

More immediate is another Black-Douglas contention, namely, that because of the size and scope of corporate operations, corporations can and do make rules having the effect of legislation.[13]

This is an indisputable sociological fact. It was the subject of judicial scrutiny in *Plessy* v. *Ferguson*,[14] giving

13. Justice Douglas—quite rightly—in *Bell* v. *Maryland* added a few appendices to his concurring opinion, as we said. Because argument had been made that the restaurant owner had a right to choose his own customers and associates, one of these memoranda pointed out that the owner was not a person, but a corporation; that, indeed, most owners of property offering facilities to the public were corporations; that a corporation was not a "natural person" whose "personal right" was infringed when forced to open its lunch counter to people of all races, and he attached a list of corporate business establishments involved in Negro "sit-in" cases before the Supreme Court in the 1962 and 1963 terms. Of twenty cases involved, two were partnerships or private proprietorships; the others were chiefly chain operations with thousands of stockholders. Justice Douglas said further, "Affirmance would make corporate management the arbiter of one of the deepest conflicts in our society: corporate management could then enlist the aid of state police, state prosecutors, and state courts to force apartheid on the community they served" (*Bell* v. *Maryland*, at p. 880). As Douglas saw it, if the Court did not legislate, corporate managements could and would use their commercial organizations as institutions, and their notions of the probable greatest profit as their philosophy.

rise to the now discarded requirement of "separate but
equal" accommodation for Negroes, first on public car-
riers. Internal rules and regulations made by corporate
managements (like those involved in *Plessy* v. *Ferguson*)
for running their businesses can and do vitally affect the
lives of their employees, their agents, their suppliers, their
customers, and the public. Employees are, of course, protected—if they so choose—by the countervailing power
arising from rights of organization and collective bar-
gaining guaranteed under the Taft-Hartley Act and the
rulings of the National Labor Relations Board, though
that should not and does not exclude protection of them
as individuals under the Fourteenth Amendment should
corporate rules, resting on economic power, impair their
rights. The other three categories, notably suppliers and
customers, are not as a rule protected by any organization giving them "countervailing power." Danger that
intracorporate rules governing the operations of the business might deprive Negroes of equal protection was the
focus of Justice Douglas's discussion in *Bell* v. *Maryland*
—but he barely scratched one surface of a huge area.

Take, for example, the case of consumer credit terms
in the automobile-finance business. It is statistically prov-
able that great numbers of American citizens can have
and hold jobs only if they have automobiles taking them
to and from work. It is also a statistical fact that about
90% of all automobiles are bought on credit. It is also
true that the great bulk of automobile-finance credit is

14. *Plessy* v. *Ferguson,* 163 US 537 (1897). The Court had under
examination claim that a Negro was denied equal protection of the
laws because he was not allowed to ride in a railway carriage reserved
for whites. Corporate regulations as well as state laws offered to
Negroes "Jim Crow" accommodations.

handled by a very few large corporations under more or less standard terms and guidelines dictated by them. Admittedly credit-worthiness is a somewhat delicate matter, difficult of reduction to absolute terms. Under these circumstances, a finance company regulation denying credit to one category of applicants or discriminating against others can, quite simply, deny applicants access to their jobs and their living as well as to easier lives.

Unlike the situation in *Bell* v. *Maryland,* or *Shelley* v. *Kraemer,*[15] the corporation does not have to call in local police or courts to enforce its regulations: the customer simply does not get the service. No pretense can be made that governmental mechanism of any kind was called in to prevent him getting it. Is it open to serious doubt that the judicial revolution already requiring elimination of discrimination against Negroes will eventually reach discriminatory practice in other fields?

At risk of being accused of a flight of fancy, I suggest a further possibility. Increasingly, information on men is being accumulated for credit purposes—and for employment purposes. Under corporation-made "programs," it is increasingly stored in machines called "computers." Insertion of an item into these machines may affect or wreck a career, low or high, or a journey at home or abroad. The computer can erect walls, unbreakable though invisible. It may block a man in any number of directions—from obtaining a license to drive a motorcar to getting a credit card or a job.

15. *Shelley* v. *Kraemer,* 334 US 1 (1948). An action to prevent a Negro from taking title to a house because of a covenant prohibiting its sale to Negroes was struck down by the Supreme Court on the ground that the state courts violated the Fourteenth Amendment by enforcing such a covenant.

It is to be presumed that an individual wrong caused by combined corporate and computer machinery will be dealt with under normal rules of tort liability. Should this happen, "equal protection of the laws" will be provided by normal processes.[16] Active development of law in this field has been, and still is, the best protection against unfair extension of the power of judicial legislation granted the federal courts. We cannot, however, ignore the possibility that state law may not adequately deal with the field. In that case, we must contemplate a still-greater extension of the Supreme Court's power—consonant with its duty of providing "equal protection."

The capacity of computer operations to impinge on human life has yet to be fully imagined, still less realized. But it already exists.[17] Take a single situation, presently

16. Even so, remedy through tort action is not a reason for denying habeas corpus. For example, a person may be imprisoned in a private hospital. He may have a fully adequate remedy by action for false imprisonment. This is not, however, reason for denying habeas corpus. A money judgment is not adequate reparation for loss of liberty.

17. In 1939, the Temporary National Economic Committee (TNEC), constituted by Congress, investigated concentration of economic power. Part 10 of its hearings related to intercompany agreements between life insurance companies (pp. 643–648). It developed that the Association of Life Insurance Medical Directors maintained what is known as the Medical Information Bureau (M.I.B.), in which was collected all the information derived from medical examination of individuals seeking life insurance. In 1939 it had records of approximately 6,700,000 people (p. 4637).

It is computerized today. The number has immensely increased.

In 1966 a Task Force under the chairmanship of Dr. Carl Kaysen completed a report (available through the Bureau of the Budget), *The Report of the Task Force on the Storage of and Access to Government Statistics*. It proposed a National Data Center, though its thrust was statistical. Yet, in Kaysen's words, "for the data center to achieve its intended purpose, the material in it must identify indi-

in rapid development. Intercommunication of machines by machines with machines—that is, between computer systems—is already in operation. Let us suppose that the computer systems presently used by the great New York banks are made to intercommunicate with the computer systems presently being used in other financial or consumer-credit corporations (many of them owned by these same banks). Add to the credit data they store, the budget of computer information regarding a man's record for, let us say, safe automobile driving, previous satisfactory employment, and the like. In fear of overstating, I do not add the possibility of intercommunication between these and the machines presently scrutinizing federal income-tax returns or classifying F.B.I. records, though that possibility cannot be altogether ruled out. Then let us suppose a very simple case. A man traveling on an airline credit card is abroad or away from

---

vidual respondents in some way, by Social Security number for individuals, or an analogous code number now used within the Census for business enterprises called the Alpha number. These numbers need in turn to be keyed to a list of respondents which identifies them by name and address within the data center itself," or "within the actual data collecting agencies." (See Carl Kaysen, "Data Banks and Dossiers," *The Public Interest,* Number 7, Spring 1967, pp. 52–56.)

The Bureau of Internal Revenue maintains a computer data bank designed to cover practically all income-tax returns. Kaysen himself believes (p. 58) that the Congress might specifically prohibit the inclusion in the proposed data bank of dossier information—that is, information in which the specific identity of the individual is essential for its purposes rather than a file of data for statistical purposes.

Of course, nothing prevents the accumulation of private dossier material—as, for instance, the Medical Information Bureau information and the files maintained by great bureaus. Separate public agencies maintain dossier files for police purposes. I feel that the proliferation and increase of these banks can no longer be prevented.

home. The computer complex picks up a piece of information—it may be false—that on one occasion he
issued a check that bounced, or he failed to pay an in-
stallment contract on time. It grinds out the conclusion
that his airline credit card should no longer be honored,
and, also by computer, transmits this ruling to every airline office in the country. He is duly denied credit for a
ticket home; he is unlikely to be able to obtain money
at any bank. He is left hanging. He, of course, is totally
unaware of the internal operation of the machine. All he
knows is that the credit operation on which his voyage
has been constructed has shut down on him.

The computer-transmitted facts may be true but so
long lived down that they should have become irrelevant.
Or they may be false, inserted by error or malice or by
a slip in the machine. Even after getting out of his travel
predicament, he has no ready way of discovering what
the difficulty is, of demanding some sort of hearing
thereon, or any readily practicable way of clearing the
record.

Is it too farfetched to suggest that the time may come
when a writ of habeas corpus will be granted against the
possessor or operator of a computer? I do not think so.
Imprisoned within the computer is an extension of the
man—his record and reputation, his ability to get a job
or secure credit. If the machine is favorable, he is en-
franchised in this organized world; if unfavorable, he may
be barred from great segments of it. Prison limits, even
at common law, were not necessarily fixed by stone walls
or iron bars.

But there are corporate developments proceeding rapidly where men are left unprotected by current legal evolution. A spectacular one is the growing scope of private pension trust funds designed to provide retirement pensions and other benefits for workers. Most corporations have such funds, either by their own wish or because such funds are required as "fringe benefits" connected with their wage arrangements with labor unions. The subject was pioneered at the Columbia Law School by Dr. Paul Harbrecht (now Dean of the Detroit Law School) in his book *Pension Funds and Economic Power*.[18]

Now pension trust agreements, while beneficial, can also be tremendously oppressive. They can, for example, provide that the worker who leaves or changes his job sacrifices a large part of the payments made into the fund as part of his compensation. They can make it difficult if not impossible for an older man to get a job—because the payments required under the pension trust arrangement become greater as he grows older. Conversely, they can increase the sacrifice of accumulated pension rights if an older man leaves his job to take another one. A pension trust can thus tie a man to a job by economic pressure, or prevent a man from getting a job by like pressure. The subject is being discussed at both state and federal levels. It is, I think, possible that legislation may cover the field—but there is no guarantee of that. At the pace at which these pension trusts are increasing, in coverage, amount, and impact, we could easily be faced with a situation in which whole classes of individuals, through no fault or consent of their own, are severely constricted.

18. New York, Twentieth Century Fund, 1959.

As the system becomes general—a present possibility—
"equal protection of the laws" against some of the results could well become an active question. The constitutional problem could be avoided by legislation setting
up a clearinghouse and permitting interchange of accumulated pension rights, and by permitting newcomers into
the pension funds to accept lower benefits than those
granted to beneficiaries who have contributed over a long
period of time. This is what I hope will happen. But if it
does not, how long will the exclusion or immobilization
of some workers be accepted as merely a regrettable
though irremediable consequence of corporate economic
arrangements?

The point need not be labored. Life in a modern, in-
dustrialized, intricately organized world is a reality. This
is the world of great corporations and, now, of computer
action. Neither probability nor practicality suggests re-
turn to the older, simpler organization in which multi-
tudes of individual relationships were the doors through
which men moved. Then, closing of any one door did not
materially limit freedom. Today, it is otherwise: men
move within the frameworks of great organizations and
their increasing mechanization. The rules of their mechanization are far more compulsive, binding, and privatory
than were governmental dangers to freedom premising
the Constitution's Bill of Rights. They are carried out by
artificial persons whose capacity to make them was
erected and granted by the several states in their respec-
tive corporation acts. Already, as in *Bell* v. *Maryland,*
the Supreme Court has reached the point of saying that
where the local state police or courts are called in to en-

force them (*Shelley* v. *Kraemer*), there is state action, controlled by constitutional protection. But in the case of a credit regulation, intervention of the police or the courts is not needed: the corporate rule is self-enforcing. Are we to assume in such case that the positive duty of states to maintain a system giving "equal protection of the laws" has not been infringed? The state of the present judicial revolution suggests an emerging doctrine. Rules, regulations, and practices, machine-made or otherwise, by which corporations carry on their business are, in and of themselves, subject to judicial scrutiny and, if need be, change by judicial decree under the current standards of the Fourteenth Amendment.

In an appropriate case, the Supreme Court should declare that corporate action denying "equal protection of the laws" is in essence state action, because the effectiveness of an action is derived from state power to grant the corporate-form privileges or (at least) from the state's failure to control the corporation by appropriate law—that is, inaction constituting responsible state action within the meaning of the Fourteenth Amendment. If anything is clear, it is that a state does have power to determine what a corporation of its creation shall and shall not do. It may, by statute, lay down requirements for corporate action. It can set up administrative tribunals to which any individual aggrieved may apply for summary remedy, as New York has done in the employment field. Such remedies could be made applicable to corporate action ground out by computer machines as well as by corporate officers or employees.

Far from worrying about this constitutional development, I welcome it. Corporate power has served the United States well. In substantial measure, the material prosperity of the country is due to it. Like any other power, it can be abused. A major bulwark against that abuse is the body of rules and doctrines emerging from the judicial revolution we have been examining. As a corporation lawyer, I believe these fascinating, frightening, and fantastic institutions will be strengthened rather than weakened by the application of constitutional limitations—and requirements of action—to them.

A final point is in the nature of a glance down the vista.

Business increasingly is becoming interrelated with government processes. In many states of the Union, it is illegal to drive an uninsured car. The right to drive, under proper licensing or regulation, is clear enough. The right to get insurance, so far as I am aware, does not as yet have legal sanction. It has been assumed that insurance companies would provide coverage. Yet so far as I am aware, they are entitled to choose what risks they will insure and what risks they will deny. Already, and perhaps on sound actuarial grounds, they charge discriminatory rates for teen-age drivers and for adults whose families include teen-agers. They could—as some of them are beginning to do—refuse the business altogether, or accept only selected categories of individuals whose probability of being involved in accidents they consider low. The growing number of cars on the road, the losses suffered in the casualty insurance business and appellate court acceptance of irresponsible verdicts for

losses contribute to making the business increasingly un-
attractive. In effect, the result is increasingly to make
private companies final arbiters of whether men can drive
cars. This was tolerable enough a generation ago, when
driving was a privilege and a luxury. It becomes dangerous when driving is, virtually, a necessary adjunct of life
for most citizens.

The illustration given is only one of a number of similar interrelations. In many situations, the right of an individual to enjoy quite ordinary attributes of life is made
dependent on the willingness of a private business to
attend to his needs and provide (for a price) the necessary evidence that the work was done.

Project this situation a few years. By the turn of the
century, the population of the United States will be well
over a quarter of a billion. The density of certain areas
may become very great. Large demonstration by words
is not needed to show that "equal protection of the laws"
must mean equal access to certain kinds of services. That
in turn means that many substantially private businesses
will find themselves in a position to permit or deny at will
the usual accessories of life or living. Access to the service of a chain store may be needed to keep the family
fed; to the local garage to have the brakes inspected on
the essential car; and so on through the list.

But by now the character of business is changed. It is
more than merely rendering private goods and services
for a price by a willing seller to a customer who wants to
buy. The services may not be "state services" in the ordinary sense; but they are projected to cardinal importance as the state increasingly recognizes, uses, and re-

quires that these services shall have been rendered in
some cases and, in others, that they shall not be denied
on request.

4. "Abstention" from Use of Judicial Power—an Illusion

The problems of the field of economic organization—
like those of the field of local government—are immense
and growing. Other similar problems are certain to
emerge. Conceivably, the federal courts could avoid them
by exercising their ancient power of "federal question
abstention" on a number of hallowed grounds. Abstention
ordinarily is invoked (a) on the ground that the problem
raised is essentially political or (b) to avoid unnecessary
constitutional adjudication or (c) to allow state courts
to determine issues where the state law appears unclear.
In view of the many massive legal questions now presented and of the unforeseeable impact of decisions, one
can sympathize with those who feel that the Supreme
Court should be astute enough not to decide many of
the issues presented and to be presented.

All of us are aware of the late Justice Frankfurter's
solution reached in *Railroad Commission* v. *Pullman
Company*—that of stepping out of the legislative power
position so far as possible and in other matters leaving
the problem of providing "equal protection of the laws,"
save in matters of judicial procedure, to the political

mechanisms of government.[19] Avoidance of tough questions is indeed part of established judicial procedure, but it is increasingly in disfavor, as pointed out in an elaborate note-article published in the *Harvard Law Review* for January, 1967.[20] In my judgment, avoidance is not now possible. A corollary to the first law of power (that it always replaces chaos) is an implacable rule. Power cast aside without provision for its further exercise almost invariably destroys the abdicating power holder—as, for example, Shakespeare's King Lear found out when he improvidently abandoned his power, and was promptly crushed.[21] Conceivably, the Supreme Court might have avoided assuming the power position in the first place— but it cannot renounce it now. It has entered, created, and accepted a field of responsibility. Elements in that field might wreck the Court were it now to desert the function it has assumed. The picket lines directed against municipal governments (as in Louisville, Kentucky) would then be turned on the Supreme Court itself.

Obviously, the first duty of the Court is to resolve the specific case before it. The second—in this context a

19. *Baker* v. *Carr.*

20. Vol. 80, No. 3, pp. 604 ff.

21. Act 1, Scene 1.
"*Lear.* Meantime we shall express our darker purpose.
    Give me the map there. Know that we have divided
    In three our kingdom. And 'tis our fast intent
    To shake all cares and business from our age,
    Conferring them on younger strengths while we
    Unburdened crawl toward death."
This abdication of power could only produce a wrecked kingdom, as Lear's Fool later points out. The Dukes quarrel; the French invade the land.

more important task—is to lay down a rule of general
application to like cases. This involves the legislative
function. Sometimes, to be sure, simple determination of
the case will include the secondary effect. In the sit-in
cases (*Bell* v. *Maryland*), two concurring members—
who in fact wanted the widest legislative effect possible
—believed the Court should have dismissed the proceedings for criminal trespass and said, in Justice Douglas's
language:

Were we today to hold that segregated restaurants, whose
racial policies were enforced by a State, violated the Equal
Protection Clause, all restaurants would be on an equal foot-
ing and the reasons given in this and most of the companion
cases for refusing service to Negroes would evaporate.[22]

But simple determination that a school is segregated and
should not be, or that this legislature is badly apportioned,
does not desegregate the school or reapportion the legislature. More often, the reason given for the disposition
of the case has more legislative effect than the *ratio
decidendi*. Certainly this was true in the reapportionment cases (as, for example, in *Reynolds* v. *Sims*). In the
school segregation cases, the problem has been and now
is to give effect to the principles enunciated in *Brown* v.
Topeka. In a pending case, a district court judge, required to draw a decree for the desegregation of schools
in a number of consolidated cases, sought outside guidance. He discovered that the Department of Health, Education, and Welfare had issued a document containing

22. *Bell* v. *Maryland*, p. 246.

III

THE REDISTRIBUTION OF POWER

1. Power and Its Dialogue

An invariable result of revolution is a sudden concentration of power. This is as true of revolutions mandated by a constitutional provision such as the Fourteenth Amendment and conducted by courts as of more violent forms. To achieve their objective, there must be capacity to state the goal, develop the philosophy, set up the legislation, and draw the appropriate decrees. This is the position in which the Supreme Court today finds itself—a position, let me repeat, entirely legitimate in our constitutional system.

Yet it poses a second question with which every revolution has had to cope. Concentration of power must eventually be devolved on supporting institutions. Where revolutions are not constitutional, and institutional development is not indicated in advance, the results may be explosive, not to say disorderly. The French revolution-

ary authority had its Thermidor liquidating Robespierre
and leading later to its 18th Brumaire and the beginning
of the Napoleonic system. A familiar solution has been
a dictatorship which promptly sets to work organizing the
institutions which will maintain its regime after the immediate power holders are gone. A somewhat similar
process has been going on in the Soviet Union since the
death of Stalin. Some rearrangement seems essential to
me if the Supreme Court is to survive.[1]

Happily, the United States has a very well-developed
philosophy, vigorous institutions, and can devise orderly
solutions. It needs no Thermidors.

I attempt here to suggest one method of approach, not
because it is necessarily the right or only one, but to
stimulate thinking along this line.

The necessity of tackling the problem now rather than
later should be self-evident. Two observations may help
to guide one's thinking.

First, the revolutionary process (in this case mandated
by the current interpretation of the Constitution) arises
essentially from lack of adequate legislation.

The restaurant sit-in case (*Bell* v. *Maryland*) here used

1. Signs are not wanting that crisis is developing in the situation of
the Supreme Court. Thirty-four states have adopted the call for a
constitutional convention, designed to amend the federal Constitution.
Its primary intent is to propose a measure, sponsored by Senator
Everett M. Dirksen, of Illinois, aimed at overruling the rule of *Baker*
v. *Carr,* the "one man–one vote" ruling. The suggestion is that the
federal Constitution be so amended as to permit representation for
localities, irrespective of population. The Congress will have to call
such a constitutional convention, and it is evident that there will be
Congressional opposition. Obviously, the result of a constitutional
convention might enter areas other than those proposed by Senator
Dirksen.

as a case study would never have been brought, and the decision need never have been made, had the State of Maryland passed the antidiscrimination laws which in fact it later did adopt. Perhaps the decision would have been unnecessary had the Congress of the United States already adopted the Civil Rights Act of 1965—which was actually passed a year and a half after *Bell* v. *Maryland*. Had the Congress—or the several states—adopted legislation governing discrimination in housing, the courts probably would not have had to deal with the problem they now must solve by a succession of decrees. If regulation arising from economic power—such as that of large corporations or great aggregates of competitors—safeguarded civil rights, judges would not have to study the principles and contrive the remedies they must unquestionably design if the vacuum is left unfilled. Chief Justice Warren and Justice Goldberg were entirely right (in *Bell* v. *Maryland*) in recommending that course to the Maryland courts, because, during the pendency of the litigation, Maryland had in fact legislated. In effect, the Maryland legislation took the place—as it should—of the *ad hoc* decree the federal courts would otherwise have had to make. Our first conclusion must be that where the vacuum has been or is in the course of being filled by regular legislative process, following the recognized political philosophy and methods of the United States, courts should take judicial notice of that fact and give fullest opportunity for its realization.

Second, where courts legislate, there is failure of the essential continuing and orderly dialogue between power and the field of its responsibility.

When a president, or a congress, or a governor, or a legislature acts, the ground must be prepared politically, and opportunity given for all interests to be heard and considered, both before and after the power holders act. In American procedure, this dialogue is more or less orderly. Hearings in committee normally precede legislation; all interested parties desiring to do so have the opportunity to speak their piece. The factual situations and probable results can be estimated in advance. Interest can be balanced and dealt with accordingly. After action has been taken, public critique and comment through the press, through local committees, through interested citizens, follows as matter of course. If the power holder has acted badly, or if the legislation is unsatisfactory, the individuals and institutions involved are politically responsible—the individuals can change their position or they can be defeated at the next election; the institutions can be modified or changed.

Little of this dialogue obtains, however, with respect to court action. True, the press can comment or criticize. In more orderly debate, law schools and law professors can criticize. This fills part of the gap. Yet essentially there is no appeal when the courts have acted; there is no compulsion on courts to take account either of the press or of the law reviews; much of the comment may never reach the judges. And Supreme Court justices are not elected: they hold office for life. Factually, the halls and publications of Columbia and other law schools are the only institutions we have for reviewing Supreme Court decisions, other than agitation, or, at worst, mobs on the streets.

Any solution sought must therefore be double in char-

acter. It should provide a channel for assuring the legislation necessary to fulfill the revolutionary mandate of the
Fourteenth Amendment (and probably also of the first
ten amendments). And it should provide a forum in
which orderly dialogue can take place between power on
one hand and those affected by its use on the other.

2. Institutionalizing Judicial Legislation

There is, I suggest, a method of doing this though no
model for equivalent action has yet been pounded out.
Seeking an analogue, the most useful one I can find is
that of the Council of Economic Advisers set up by the
Employment Act of 1946.[2] The analogue is far from
close, but in fundamentals it is useful. There, the United
States was faced with the problem of economic power,
great parts of which had come into the hands of the
federal government. Particularly, it came to appear that
the combination of monetary power (located in the Federal Reserve Board) and fiscal policy applied through the
federal budget, together with certain other cognate federal powers, went far in determining the level of employment and prosperity of the United States. In 1946, no
recognized standards had been set down for the use of
that power—and only the most disorderly dialogue existed for determination or revision of its use.

In these circumstances, through the patient genius of
Senator Paul Douglas, of Illinois, an institution was
worked out which has now become classic in American

2. 15 USCA §1021, §1025.

economic administration. The Council of Economic Advisers was created, along with a joint congressional committee and the requirement of an economic report. Its effect was to place responsibility for action where it belonged—in that case, not on courts, but on the executive branch, to propose, and on the Congress, where necessary, to legislate. Simultaneously, it set up an orderly dialogue by requiring an economic report from the President, its reference to a joint committee of the House and Senate, and hearings thereon. Like all institutions, the Council of Economic Advisers took time to establish itself in the public conscience and confidence. It has done so. Debates on measures to assure adequate functioning of the American economic system proceed in regular course. Properly, problems were transferred from mere protest against unsatisfactory conditions on the street to a forum where desired results could be stated and measures proposed. Orderly critique of measures previously taken could be had and their modification or change could proceed in accordance with the regularly constituted political institutions in a democracy.

Briefly, I seek something of the sort in the constitutional situation with which we are now faced, though, as noted, the solution must be somewhat different in application.

Let us suppose that the President be directed to transmit to the Congress a report—it might be called "The Report on Realization of Constitutional Rights." (May I add the hope that it will not be in January of each year; the twin reports on the "State of the Union" and on the American economy already required in that month are enough to sink any President for the previous two months.) It should set forth a review of the areas in which effective realization of constitutional rights and, particularly, "equal protection of the laws" appear to be defective and should recommend a program for remedying the defects as the President may deem necessary or desirable.

There might be created in the Executive Office of the President, a "Council of Constitutional Advisers," composed of three or five members, appointed by the President by and with the advice and consent of the Senate. Each of these should be a person who, as a result of training, experience, and attainment, is exceptionally qualified to analyze and interpret constitutional developments, to appraise programs and activities of the federal government and of the states, and to formulate and recommend policies to promote the effective realization of constitutional rights.

If the experience of the Council of Economic Advisers is any guide, the members of the Constitutional Council would be professors of law, men with judicial experience, men with legislative experience, and men with social awareness.

The duties of the Council should be:

1. to assist and advise the President in the preparation of his report on constitutional rights;

2. to gather timely and authoritative information concerning current constitutional developments in perspective, to analyze and interpret such information in the light of a policy of active realization of constitutional rights, to determine whether developments or trends are

interfering or likely to interfere with such realization, to compile and subscribe to the presidential studies relating thereto;

3. to appraise the various programs of the federal government for the purpose of determining the extent to which such programs are contributing—and the extent to which they are not contributing—to the achievement of such realization and to make recommendations to the President with respect thereto;

4. to make and furnish such studies, reports, and recommendations with respect to federal constitutional policy and legislation as the President may request and, on request, to make similar studies and recommendations for the governors or state legislatures as these may request;

5. to make and furnish such studies, reports, and recommendations with respect to constitutional rights as the Supreme Court may request, and, upon its request, to act as master for the purpose of determining and making recommendations as to decrees.

There might be established by like legislation, a joint congressional committee, to be composed of, say, eight members of the Senate and eight members of the House of Representatives, the majority party to be represented by five members and the minority by three.

This committee should make continuing study of matters relating to constitutional rights, should hold hearings on the report of the President with respect to each of the main recommendations made by the President in that report, and should have power to employ attorneys and other experts to assist it.

The right of the joint congressional committee to hold hearings should not prejudice the right of the Council of Constitutional Advisers to hold hearings on any constitutional question on its own behalf, reporting to the President, to the joint congressional committee, and to the Supreme Court where requested. Such reports might contain recommendations for legislation to be submitted to the Congress, and in appropriate case to the governments of the several states.

The double-barreled impact of such legislation will not go unnoticed. It is, first, a mandate to the President, with the Constitutional Council as expert adviser, to review the situation annually, and, where legislation is necessary, to propose it. In other words, it is a mechanism by which legislation can be proposed before, and not after, the Supreme Court is forced to assume the responsibility. The institution is also adapted to gathering the kind of data and material on which legislation can be founded—to work out the conflicts in the Congress instead of in the courts, to be ahead instead of behind the kind of situation with which the Supreme Court has been forced to deal for the last decade through judicial legislation.

Its second effect is to set up a forum, which under this suggestion can be either the Council of Constitutional Advisers or the joint congressional committee, wherein dialogue can take place between power and those affected by it. To balance or canalize the work of protest committees and press denunciations, and indeed to provide publicity for situations needing remedy, a forum would thus be provided. Absence of such a forum is one

major difficulty in the current situation. Those prejudiced
by state inaction or by oppressive state action or by oppressive action by economic concentrates would know
where next to go. It is entirely true, as Justice Frankfurter
remarked, that many wrongs arising from a political or
economic system cannot readily be remedied by judicial
action—political action is really required. But, in the absence of any readily available place in which it may be
sought, the only alternatives are the courts and the streets
—and, in some cases, only the latter.

Access to the courts is itself time consuming and can
be immensely expensive. As of April, 1967, two committees, one operating under the auspices of the American
Bar Association, the other established, I am told, at the
insistence of the President of the United States, are presently functioning in the field. Neither has official standing; neither is adequately financed; both are wrestling
with the failure of constitutional rights in certain parts
of the United States with totally inadequate resources.
There is also a section of the Department of Justice having to do with civil rights, though it, like the unofficial
committees, deals only with a single though important
field—that of race discrimination. Our analysis nevertheless suggests that the problems are to become far
wider than those of discrimination against Negroes, important as these are.

3. Channeling Legislative Problems toward Legislatures: Education of Local Government

Not least of the attributes here suggested for the Constitutional Council is that of acting as master, referee, or research assistant to the Supreme Court of the United States. That Court (I cannot, of course, speak for it), better than anyone else, must know the staggering burdens increasingly imposed on it.

Let us take a case now pending in the District Court of the District of Columbia—*Julius Hobson et al. v. Carl F. Hansen, Superintendent of Education in the District of Columbia* (Civil Action 8266). It stems from *Brown v. Topeka*. Because an overwhelming majority of the children in the District of Columbia schools are Negroes, the schools are *de facto* segregated. No amount of nonsensical devices—such as busing white children from one part of the District of Columbia to an otherwise wholly Negro school in another—can really remedy racial separation. So plaintiffs in the litigation (it already has accumulated some 7,000 pages of testimony) advocate a decree forcibly incorporating into the District of Columbia educational system the school administrations of a series of surrounding towns—these, of course, lie in the states of Maryland and Virginia. One of the judges of the District of Columbia court, Judge J. Skelly Wright, sitting in the Hobson case, in a lecture given at the New York University Law School [3] adverted to the problem placed be-

3. *New York University Law Review*, Vol. 40, No. 2, April, 1965, pp. 285 ff.

fore him. He indicated the enormous depth of the essential legislative problem presented. No state-created political lines, he observed, can protect the state against

the constitutional command of equal protection for its citizens or relieve the state from the obligation of providing educational opportunities for its Negro slum children equal to those provided for its white children in the affluent suburbs.

When the Supreme Court decided the first reapportionment case, *Baker* v. *Carr,* just as when it decided *Brown,* it left to the district courts the task of fashioning the remedy.[4]

If this involves dealing with the fact that white families flee to suburbs, leaving Negro and poor children within the boundaries of the city, still the courts must deal with it:

Obviously, court orders running to local officials will not reach the suburbs. Nevertheless, when political lines, rather than school district lines, shield the inequality, as shown in the reapportionment cases, courts are not helpless to act. The political thicket, having been pierced to protect the vote, can likewise be pierced to protect the education of children.[5]

Reaching across state and local lines compels regional arrangements other than relocating school districts. Local and state and county financing, educational standards, school administration, and local relations to the school system are all affected. To carry out a decree of the kind suggested by Judge Wright would involve the Court's intrusion into all these affairs, and effective orders would be far-reaching indeed.

4. Both from *ibid.,* p. 306.
5. *Ibid.,* p. 305.

Courts are organized and staffed and judges are trained to resolve cases and controversies, and decree remedies in individual cases. But where in doing that they are expected to enunciate rules applying to multitudinous situations at the same time—that is, to legislate—the problem of collecting data and arriving at a solution certainly goes beyond their ordinary function. It is unfair as well as unwise to expect from courts legislation reorganizing county and state governments, rearranging school districts, directing school superintendents how their schools should be administered, determining whether the education given is sufficiently uniform to constitute "equal protection of the laws."

The situation may be still worse when some other problems arise. A small labor union, controlling an essential service—for example, New York City transit or garbage collection or, perhaps, one day, electric light and power—has a right to strike. At some point, exercise of that right will deprive great areas of the community of the capacity to exercise liberty—may even, indeed, take from them their lives. That happened during the Transport Workers' strike in New York in January, 1966. Now a union under the Taft-Hartley Act has privileges and responsibilities placed on it by federal law, and from these rights and privileges its power is chiefly derived. Already it has been held, in *Brotherhood of Locomotive Engineers et al., Petitioners* v. *Louisville & Nashville Railroad Company*,[6] that the limits of the Fourteenth Amendment apply to some of a union's action; it may not

6. *Brotherhood of Locomotive Engineers et al., Petitioners* v. *Louisville & Nashville Railroad Company,* 370 US 908 (1962).

lawfully exclude from membership, and therefore from a job, a man who is a Negro. But its use of its power may also deprive members of the public of rights they have to life and liberty. Drawing the limitations which ought to circumscribe action by labor unions will be a legislative task of first importance—and courts ought not to be asked to do it.

Yet, as we have seen, the "equal protection" clause contains a built-in mandate to require action—as well as merely to strike down offending action. The case being stated, the courts must act or else resort to judicial abstention—hiding behind one or another device to avoid exercise of federal jurisdiction. But abstention from deciding federal—in these cases, constitutional—questions is itself a maze of judicial doctrine; see, for example, *Turner v. City of Memphis.*[7] There the lower federal courts abstained from deciding constitutional questions, and were duly overruled. Since the retirement of Justice Frankfurter, abstention has become unfashionable. In any case, while abstention may get the federal courts out of difficulty, the fundamental problem remains unsolved. This is why it is not perhaps an impertinence to set up an institution to which such questions may be referred for expert opinion, not on the facts of the case, but on the effects of any decision.

This is what a Constitutional Council of the kind suggested could do. If legislation were proposed or in progress, that fact could be suggested to the courts. Abstention to get away from a problem is one thing. Abstention to permit orderly resolution of the problem (other than

7. *Turner* v. *City of Memphis,* 369 US 350 (1962).

of individual rights in the situation) is quite different, and perhaps justifiable. If in a case the Supreme Court has to make a decree, it would have the equivalent of a committee report, presumably rendered after research of the relevant material. If, on the other hand, the Council reported that the matter was in ordinary legislative process, there would seem to be honorable reason for the courts, possibly retaining jurisdiction, to stand aside and leave the remedy to the Congress, or perhaps to the state in question, as the case might be. Specifically, it would provide a method for recommending questions essentially legislative in character to the institutions presently in existence to deal with them, backed by the political processes of the United States, and after an appropriate dialogue carried on before the Constitutional Council or the joint congressional committee.

I have not overlooked one ultimate in this situation. No matter what arrangements are set up, the case may arise in which, political processes having denied action necessary to create "equal protection of the laws," the Supreme Court must move in. From this possibility there is under the present system no escape. If by political processes, including majority votes, even taken under the "one man–one vote" rule, the majority oppresses a minority —as when a duly elected Congress passes a bill of attainder, or refuses to wrestle with a problem of civil rights—the Supreme Court not only may, but must, act. At long last, its honorable judgment must control the limitations on its action.

This the American system and the American public accepts—has accepted, indeed, by giving the Supreme

Court of the United States authority almost unknown in
judicial history. That authority obviously cannot be
stretched beyond the limits of its continued public acceptance. The Supreme Court, I suggest, might welcome
an institution such as the Constitutional Council, permitting it to use its final and reserved authority only where
conditions require it to do so. Exercise of such authority
necessarily puts the Supreme Court in politics—and sub-
jects it to a political result.

The object of the suggestion here made is to precipitate
political questions, so far as possible before rather than
after the Supreme Court enters the arena.

4. Channeling Problems of Economic Organization toward Administrative Authorities

Parallel suggestion is offered to deal with the functions of
the Supreme Court in problems of economic organization.

The legal basis for the Court's operations in this field
differs from its authority in the field of civil rights and the
organization of government. Prima facie, there is no constitutional warrant for judicial legislation in this area—
the Sherman Antitrust Act had to be elevated to quasi-
constitutional status. Yet, how the United States chooses
to organize its economic affairs is the business of the
Congress of the United States so far as interstate commerce is affected—and in other respects is the business
of the several states. There may be—there is—legitimate

reason for curbing undue or dangerous concentration of economic power. There may be—there is—solid reason for assuring that great corporate aggregations shall not use "market power" to the detriment of the public, or perhaps shall not be allowed to acquire "market power" in significant degree. But the existence of economic concentration and the acquisition of market power are not, in and of themselves, denials of "equal protection of the laws." Undue competition indeed may create more hazards than market stability. The elected representatives of the American public may so decide if they choose, and it will not be for the Supreme Court to say them "nay." Nothing in the Constitution and its amendments delegates the power of legislation in this field to the Supreme Court.

Unless, of course, under the system as it emerges the power does deprive citizens of equal protection. Such situations can arise. But it is one thing for the Court to decree a remedy when such a situation has arisen; it is quite another for it, fearing future abuse, to decree whether and where economic power shall be located. That is a political question for the voters when they elect the Congress and legislatures. If they choose to maintain or continue methods of economic organization carrying the hazard of oppression, they have a right to do so, whatever the Court may think. In any case, the political debate should revolve around the essential question, not around the power of the Supreme Court. Corporations and congressional action on antitrust laws should be the foci of discussion, not the views or power of the Supreme Court.

Danger to the Court is obvious in the current state of

affairs. Until recently, the Court had rested its ever-
widening action in the field of economic organization on
the two antitrust laws—the Sherman Act and the Clayton
Act. It stated in the *Brown Shoe Company* case that the
people of the United States had placed their faith in the
continuance of a system of free competition, even though
it might be more costly than some other. This was sound:
the Employment Act of 1946 declared the policy of the
United States to be that of fostering maximum employment, maximum production, and maximum purchasing
power under a system of free competition. There was
demonstrable, if small, lessening of competition in *Brown
Shoe Company*. But in *Federal Trade Commission* v.
Procter & Gamble, a proceeding was brought by the Federal Trade Commission to prevent acquisition by Procter
& Gamble of Clorox Company, a concern engaged in an
entirely separate field—that of manufacturing liquid
bleaches. There was no competition between the two
companies. The Court reversed a district court decision
sanctioning the merger on the ground that Procter &
Gamble was already powerful—if not dominant—in its
own field, as was Clorox in another, and that acquisition
of Clorox plus Procter's capacity to use its resources and
advertising power could give Procter market capacity in
the future to prevent other concerns from competing.
Lessening competition was not present. Undue market
power capable of forestalling potential competition *in future* became the test.[8]

8. In *Federal Trade Commission* v. *Procter & Gamble Company* (decided by the Supreme Court April 11, 1967, October Term, 1966, No.
342), the Court considered that §7 of the Clayton Act "can deal only
with probabilities, not with certainties," and thus justified a decree

Again I agree with the result as desirable legislation. But this further entry of the Court into the field of economic organization strikes me as a dubious elevation of the Court's functions. It is constitutionally mandated to become a revolutionary committee in the field of "equal protection." When called on to do so, the Court must take the political chances involved in assumption of that function. But *Federal Trade Commission* v. *Procter &*

---

enjoining merger because the firm "may substantially reduce the competitive structure of the industry by raising entry barriers and by dissuading the smaller firms from aggressively competing"—and also because Procter & Gamble, though it never had competed with Clorox, would not do so after acquiring it.

Clorox had 48.8% of the premerger liquid-bleach market. Procter was not in that market—but the Federal Trade Commission found that its purchase of Clorox eliminated it as a potential competitor. The advertising budget of Procter was ten times that of Clorox; entry into the liquid-bleach market was found to require large expenses for advertising, but Procter had resources for the purpose. The advertising capacity of Procter combined with the share of the liquid-bleach market already held by Clorox, the Federal Trade Commission thought, entailed "the reasonable probability of a substantial increase in barriers to entry and of enhancement of pricing power in the liquid bleach industry." Procter was accordingly ordered to divest itself of its holdings in Clorox.

This is a long projection into the "field of possibility"—valid as justification for precautionary legislation but somewhat speculative when it comes to a judicial decree.

An interesting comment both on *Brown Shoe Company* and on *Procter & Gamble* is found in Andrew Shonfield's *Modern Capitalism* (London, Oxford University Press, 1966, p. 327): "It is hard to imagine a British judge being called upon to decide not the question of ascertainable fact about the existence or not of monopolistic conditions in a given market, but whether a particular merger between two firms was likely *at some future date* to create conditions in an industry which would weaken the competitive process in it." And again (p. 328): "In the traditional British system there is no place for the use of the courts to further some evolving purpose of public administration. In America there is."

Gamble, without the mandate of the Fourteenth Amendment, pushes the Clayton Act into new, unlegislated ground. The Supreme Court legislated against market power because it *might* prevent future competition. Let us assume—I myself believe—that some such legislation is needed. Let us further assume that some delegation of power to a tribunal other than the Congress will be essential when such legislation is passed. The Federal Trade Commission exists for such purpose. But it is not clear that the Supreme Court, even with a Federal Trade Commission opinion as a base, using its own conceptions of desirable economic organization, can enter the field itself and undertake the job.

The Congress of the United States exists. Through the years it has been at least as good if not a better synthesis of the desires of the United States.

Contrast the issue raised by *Federal Trade Commission* v. *Procter & Gamble* with the issue which would be raised if, let us say, one or more great corporations undertook to interfere directly with the liberties, privileges, and persons of individuals. Let us suppose that a corporation undertakes to collect a data-bank of information on individuals it considered to be undesirable, violating the right of privacy, either because these individuals were obnoxious to it or because they held doctrines the corporation's executives disliked. (Some corporations have done this.) Obviously, the economic power of the corporation is here used directly to assault an individual or group of them. In such case, a square constitutional question would be raised: Did the corporation in question conspire to violate the individual's rights or deprive

him of equal protection of the laws? If existing legislation
were insufficient, the Court, on the ground given in *Bell*
v. *Maryland* might utilize its reserve revolutionary power
under the Fourteenth Amendment and decree a remedy.

Questions of economic organization differ markedly
from those raised in the school segregation cases or the
"one man–one vote" cases. They present the problem, not
of violation of right, but of danger. This is matter for
precautionary legislation rather than for remedying a
denial of equal protection. Normally, problems of economic power do not call for a Council of Constitutional
Advisers. Rather, they call for examination of existing
laws governing economic organization itself.

My suggestion in this field would be that the Federal
Trade Commission be given an additional function. It
should be directed to report on such questions to the
Congress. When advocated by President Woodrow Wilson
and first established by the Congress in 1914, the commission was expected to defend against monopoly. The
"New Freedom" under whose aegis it was constituted
aimed at just this result. Fear of undue economic concentration was one of the battle cries of the campaign of
1912. The thinking of the Supreme Court of the United
States rather markedly approximates the political attitudes
of that time.

The Federal Trade Commission could be directed by
the Congress to carry on a steady review of the problems
of economic concentration and organization in the rapidly changing context of American development. It can,
and should, review the problems of concentration of
economic power, of market power, of the mechanical

centralization of power, and of the impacts on competition and business and individual capacity to enter or leave markets. It can and should be charged with proposing legislation. It should work in conjunction with the Council of Economic Advisers, whose measures are supposed to maintain a system of free competition.[9]

Wherever the federal courts are asked to deal with the economic organization of an industry, or with extensions of market power and cognate questions, they should refer the problem to the Federal Trade Commission for a report. In these cases, reference might be made directly by federal district courts, where antitrust proceedings are begun. After a finding of illegality, the device of using the Federal Trade Commission as a master to propose a decree could be availed of. Where the Federal Trade Commission foresees danger not dealt with by existing legislation, it should report to the Congress and the President, asking for legislation.

There is not, I suggest, danger that the United States will be misgoverned by a revolutionary committee known as the "Supreme Court." The danger lies deeper.

9. Under the Employment Act of 1946 (15 USCA §1021), the Council of Economic Advisers, in theory, has two objectives: to maintain conditions offering useful employment for all seeking to work, and to maintain conditions promoting maximum employment, production, and purchasing power—but these conditions are to be created "in a manner calculated to foster and promote free competitive enterprise."

As economic development proceeds, it may appear (or may be true now) that "free competitive enterprise" may be inconsistent with either or both of the other objectives. This fact has not yet been taken into account by politicians, and few economists (J. K. Galbraith excepted) have been willing to deal with it.

It inheres in the nature of that "revolutionary progress" pinpointed by Justice Abe Fortas and quoted in the first of these chapters. "Revolutionary" is an overworked word, meaning drastic changes of some sort. Nevertheless, revolution of any sort implies change in the functioning of existing institutions if not in the institutions themselves. More specifically, it involves change in the power structure. Such change (as these essays perhaps have shown) is going forward rapidly, and the Supreme Court has, as Justice Fortas observed, been the active agent of such change. Change is justified because impelled by a combination of material, mechanical, and economic growth moving at breakneck speed, plus an enhanced social awareness of the impact of this on individual life. The result of Court-made breakthroughs has been salutary. The danger is that they constitute the Supreme Court a variety of benevolent dictator.

Acquiescent acceptance of any benevolent dictatorship in time deadens the public to its responsibility for apprehending needs and dangers and demanding that their elected executives and legislators take appropriate measures. As John Stuart Mill observed, it compromises the future. Nonacceptance, on the other hand, piles up political pressures focused against the institution itself. Judicial legislation is not a substitute for political and legislative institutional processes. The will of the most enlightened Court is not the same as the will of the elected representatives of the people, and may cease to be the will of the people itself. Acceptance of its mandates based on respect for the Court is not the same as acceptance of active laws commanding popular assent after political debate.

Awareness of the dangers and needs requires continuing statement of them and confronting them as problems to be dealt with by legislation.

INDEX

Marshall, John, Chief Justice, 26
Marx, Karl, 30
Maryland, state of: antidiscrim-
ination laws, 57. *See also*
Bell v. *Maryland*
Medical Information Bureau. *See*
Association of Life Insur-
ance Medical Directors
Medicare, 8, 8n
Mergers. *See* Antitrust law
Mill, John Stuart, 77
Minneapolis Railway Company
v. *Beckwith*, 33, 35, 39
Modern Capitalism (Shonfield),
73n
Monopolies. *See* Antitrust law
Montgomery Ward & Co., 8n

National Association for the
Advancement of Colored
People, 53n
National Data Center, 42n
National Labor Relations Board,
32, 40
Naturalized citizens, loss of cit-
izenship, 25
New York, state of: apportion-
ment in, 19n, 20–22; employ-
ment legislation, 47
New York Stock Exchange, 30
New York University Law
School, 65

Pension funds, 45–46
*Pension Funds and Economic
Power* (Harbrecht), 45
Plato, *Republic,* 4
Plessy v. *Ferguson,* 40, 40n
Population increase, 49
Poverty, war against, 8, 8n
Power; concentration of in the
Supreme Court, 26; eco-

nomic, 6, 29–50, 71; judicial,
50–65; laws of, 3–10, 27;
legislative, 3–28; redistribu-
tion of, 27, 55–78
Privacy, right to, 74
Procter & Gamble, and antitrust
law, 72, 72n
Public accommodations, desegregation of, 40, 40n

Race discrimination. *See* Educa-
tion, desegregation of; Pub-
lic accommodations, deseg-
regation of; "Separate but
equal" doctrine; Sit-in cases
Radio Corporation of America,
8n
Railroad Commission v. *Pullman
Company,* 50
Reapportionment cases. *See* Ap-
portionment
Recession of 1956, 31n
Religion, freedom of, 11, 38
Report of the Task Force on the
Storage of and Access to
Government Statistics, 42n
Republic (Plato), 4
Reynolds v. *Sims,* 19n, 21n, 52
Robespierre, Maximilien de, 56

Savings, personal, 37
Schneider v. *Rusk,* 25
School desegregation, 10–15, 52–
53, 65, 66
Scott v. *Germano,* 21n
Securities and Exchange Com-
mission, 32
"Separate but equal" doctrine,
14, 40, 40n
"Separation of powers" doctrine,
5, 17
Shelley v. *Kraemer,* 41, 47

Sherman Antitrust Act, 23, 24, 70, 72
Shonfield, Andrew, 73n
"Sit-in" cases, 34, 39n, 52, 56–57. *See also Bell* v. *Maryland*
Slander, law of, 25
Slavery, 6
Smith, Adam, 4
Soviet Union, 56
Speech, free. *See* Freedom of speech
Spencer, Herbert, 6n
Stalin, 56
Standard Oil of New Jersey, 30n
States, the, channeling of legislative problems toward, 65–70
Stewart, Potter, Justice, 19n, 21n
Stock, distribution of, 31
Stockholders, 36, 37
Stone, Harlan, 33
Strike, right to, 67
Supreme Court: abstention from decision and decree-making, 12, 12n, 18, 50–54; as a benevolent dictator, 77; and controls over American business, 23–24; burden imposed on, 65; concentration of power in, 26, 55, 56; extension of power, 42; and problems of economic organization, 70, 73; as a revolutionary committee, 10, 27; as senior holder of legislative power, 3–28; and "separation of powers" doctrine,

5, 17; unprecedented power of, 70
Sutton's case, 33

Taft-Hartley Act, 40, 67
Taxation: computer data bank, 43n; "negative income tax," 8; reinsurance tax, 33–34
Technical and scientific change in the U.S., 7n
Temporary National Economic Committee (TNEC), 42n
Tennessee, state of: apportionment, 15–19
Tort liability, 42, 42n
Transport Workers' strike, New York, 1966, 67
Travia v. *Lomenzo*, 21, 21n
Trial, right to, 11
Turner v. *City of Memphis*, 68

Unions. *See* Labor unions
U.S. Industries, Inc., 8n
U.S. v. *E. I. Dupont de Nemours & Company*, 23n
United States v. *Jefferson County Board of Education*, 53n

Warren, Earl, Chief Justice, 10, 13, 14, 57
Wealth of Nations (Smith), 4
Wheeling Steel Company v. *Glander*, 34
Wilson, President Woodrow, 75
WMCA v. *Lomenzo*, 20n
Wright, Judge J. Skelly, 65, 66

Xerox Corporation, 8n